GUITAR
PRAISE & WORSHIP
Level One

SONGBOOK

Shawnee Press, Inc.
1107 17th Avenue South • Nashville, TN 37212

Visit Shawnee Press Online at **www.shawneepress.com/songbooks**

How to Use this book
and enhanced Split-Track CD

The included CD makes use of split tracks. What this means is the singer is recorded on the left channel and the guitar on the right. Therefore, you have the capability of muting either one or the other while still hearing the rest of the instruments. This is very useful in the rehearsal and/or performance of songs.

For example:

By adjusting the balance control all the way to the left on your traditional CD player or stereo, you will mute the guitar. This allows you to play along with the track using live guitar.

OR:

By adjusting the balance control all the way to the right on your traditional CD player or stereo, you will mute the singer. This allows you to sing along with the track, while still hearing the guitar.

Whether muting the guitar or the singer, you can still hear all the other instruments.

By placing the balance control in the center, you will hear voice, guitar and the other instruments.

The split-track function also works if playing the CD on your PC with Windows®. Simply load your CD into the computer, and a window pops up. Choose the appropriate button, depending on the format in which you would like to hear songs played.

Your options include: Split-Track *(includes instruments and vocal),* Instruments & Guitar *(vocal muted),* or Instruments & Vocal *(guitar muted).*

NOTE: On Mac, songs will play in all formats, but you'll need to locate and play the particular MP3 which is in the format you want.

BONUS PDF FILES!

There are printable Lead Sheets (with melody, lyrics and Chord Frames) right on the CD! You may also view any lead sheet on screen while listening to the song play on your computer at the same time. The original purchaser of this book/CD may print any PDF file (lead sheet) one time. This is a non-transferable permission.

Enjoy!

Chords Reference

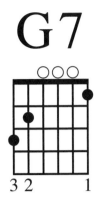 G7

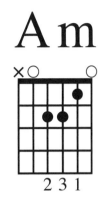 C

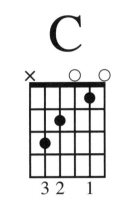 Am

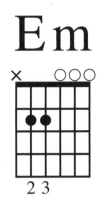 Em

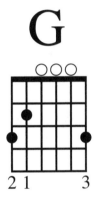 G

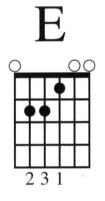 E

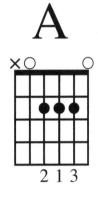 A

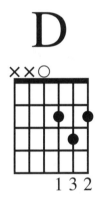 D

A5

D5

E5

Amazing Grace (My Chains Are Gone)

Words and Music by
CHRIS TOMLIN *and* **LOUIE GIGLIO**

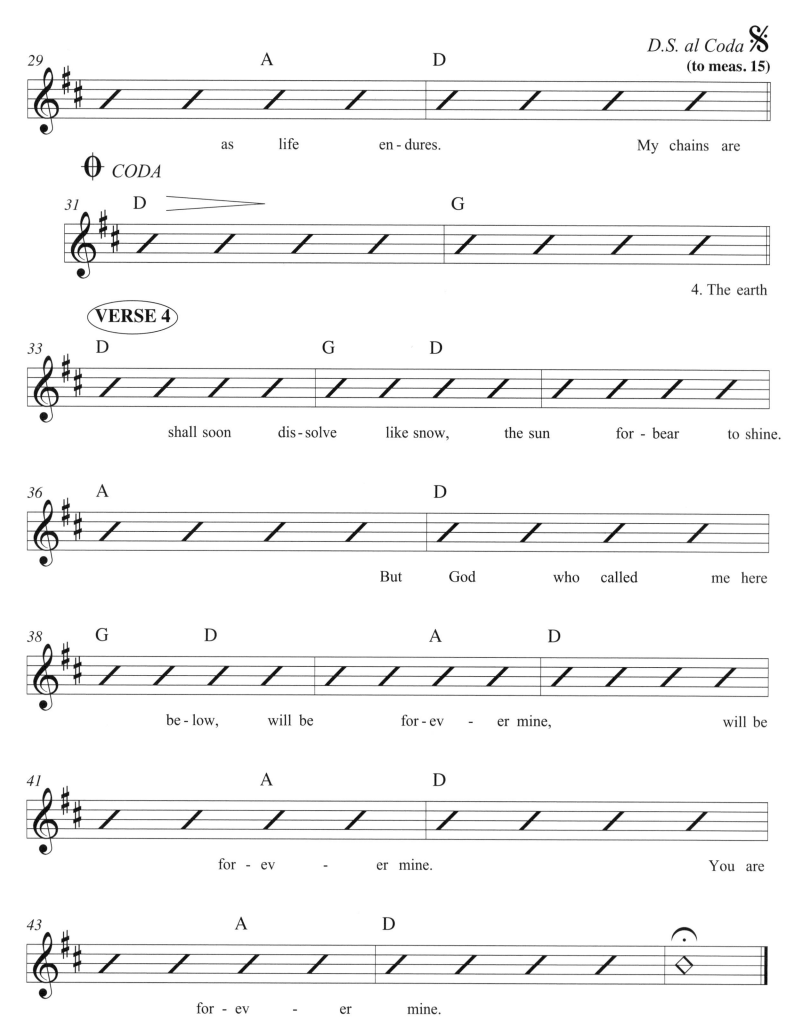

D.S. al Coda 𝄋
(to meas. 15)

29   A   D

as   life   en - dures.   My   chains   are

CODA

31   D   G

4. The earth

VERSE 4

33   D   G   D

shall soon   dis - solve   like snow,   the sun   for - bear   to shine.

36   A   D

But   God   who   called   me here

38   G   D   A   D

be - low,   will be   for - ev - er mine,   will be

41   A   D

for - ev - er mine.   You are

43   A   D

for - ev - er mine.

Hallelujah (Your Love Is Amazing)

Words and Music by
BRENTON BROWN *and* **BRIAN DOERKSEN**

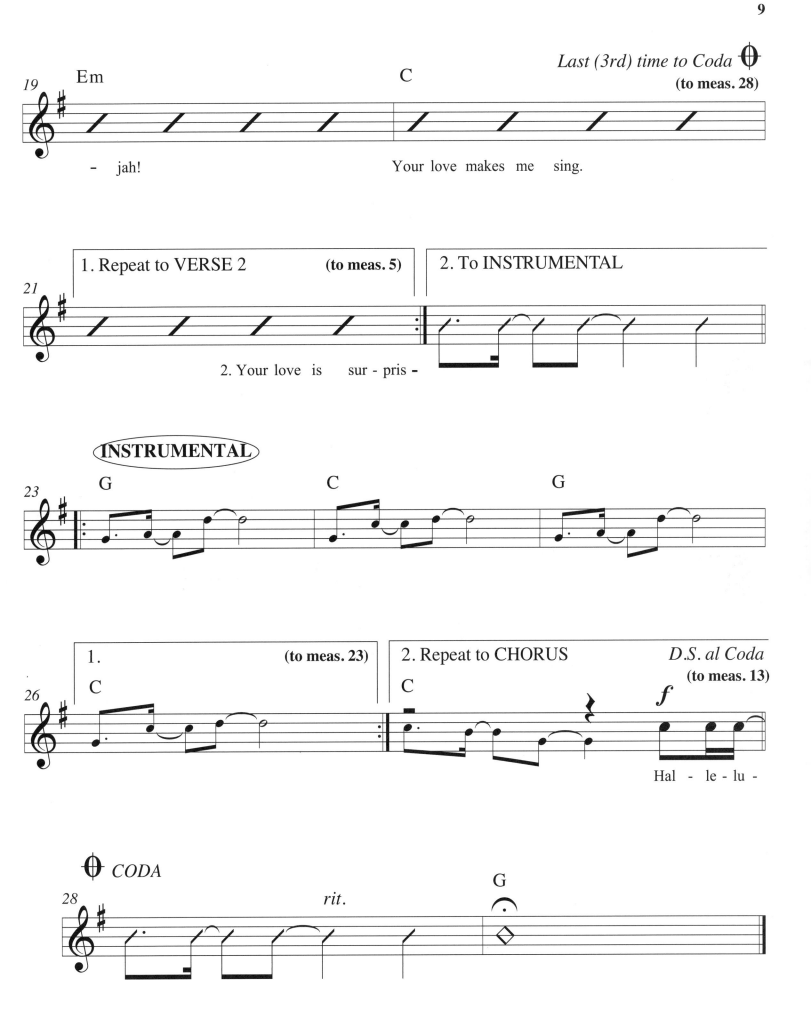

9

Breathe

Words and Music by
MARIE BARNETT

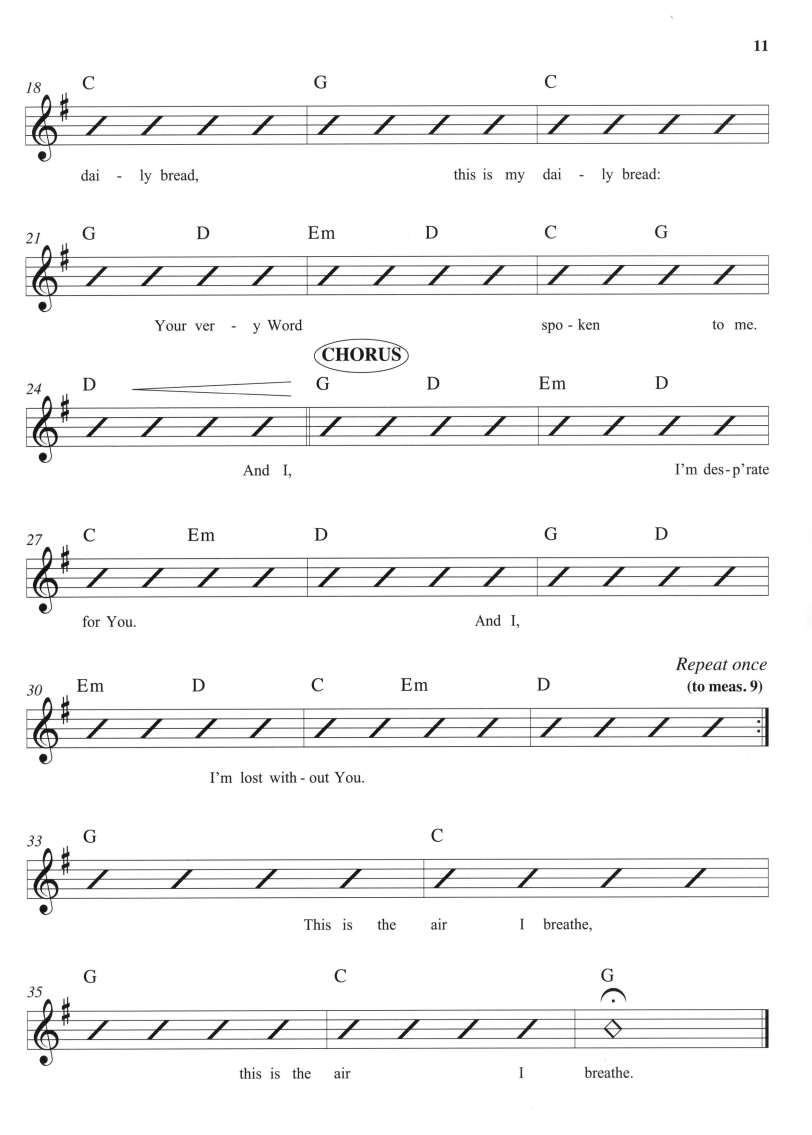

Did You Feel the Moutains Tremble?

Words and Music by
MARTIN SMITH

Acoustic Rock ♩ = 108

VERSES

1. Did you feel the moun - tains trem - ble?
2. Did you feel the peo - ple trem - ble?
(D.S.) 3. Do you feel the dark - ness trem - ble

Did you hear the o - ceans roar
Did you hear the sing - ers roar
when all the saints join in one song?

when the peo - ple rose to sing of
when the lost be - gan to sing of
And all the streams flow as one riv - er

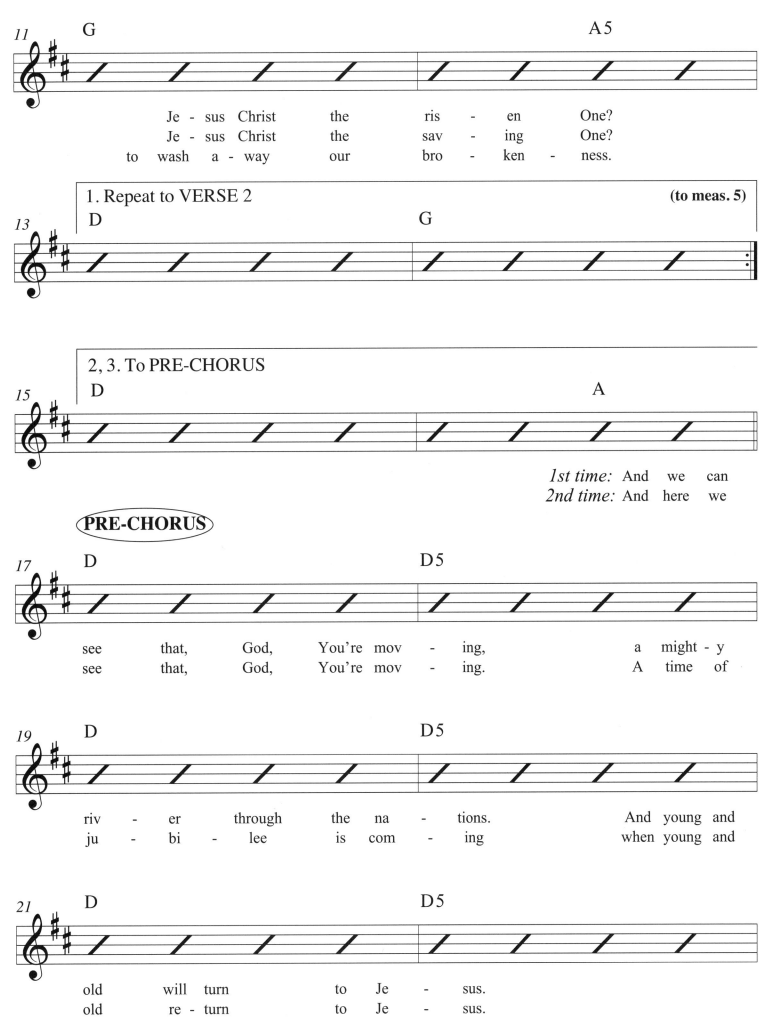

11 G   A5

Je - sus Christ   the   ris - en   One?
Je - sus Christ   the   sav - ing   One?
to wash a - way   our   bro - ken - ness.

1. Repeat to VERSE 2   **(to meas. 5)**

13 D   G

15 2, 3. To PRE-CHORUS
D   A

1st time: And   we   can
2nd time: And   here   we

PRE-CHORUS

17 D   D5

see   that,   God,   You're mov - ing,   a might - y
see   that,   God,   You're mov - ing.   A time of

19 D   D5

riv - er   through   the   na - tions.   And young and
ju - bi - lee   is   com - ing   when young and

21 D   D5

old   will   turn   to   Je - sus.
old   re - turn   to   Je - sus.

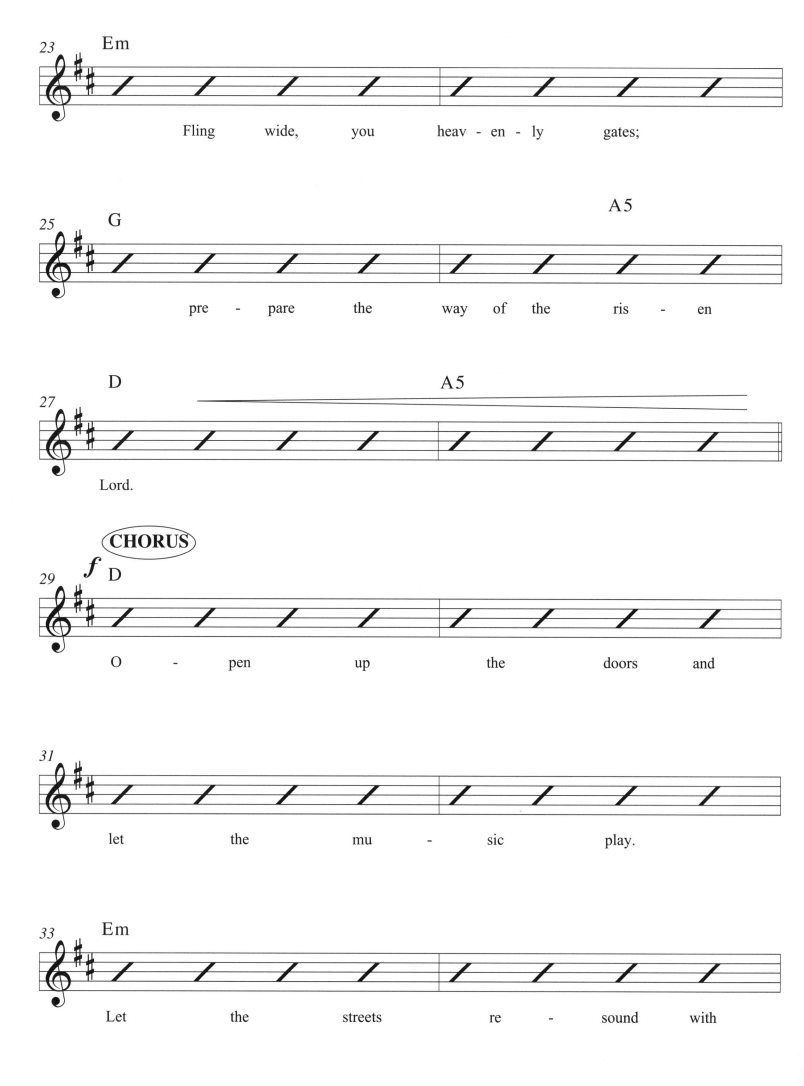

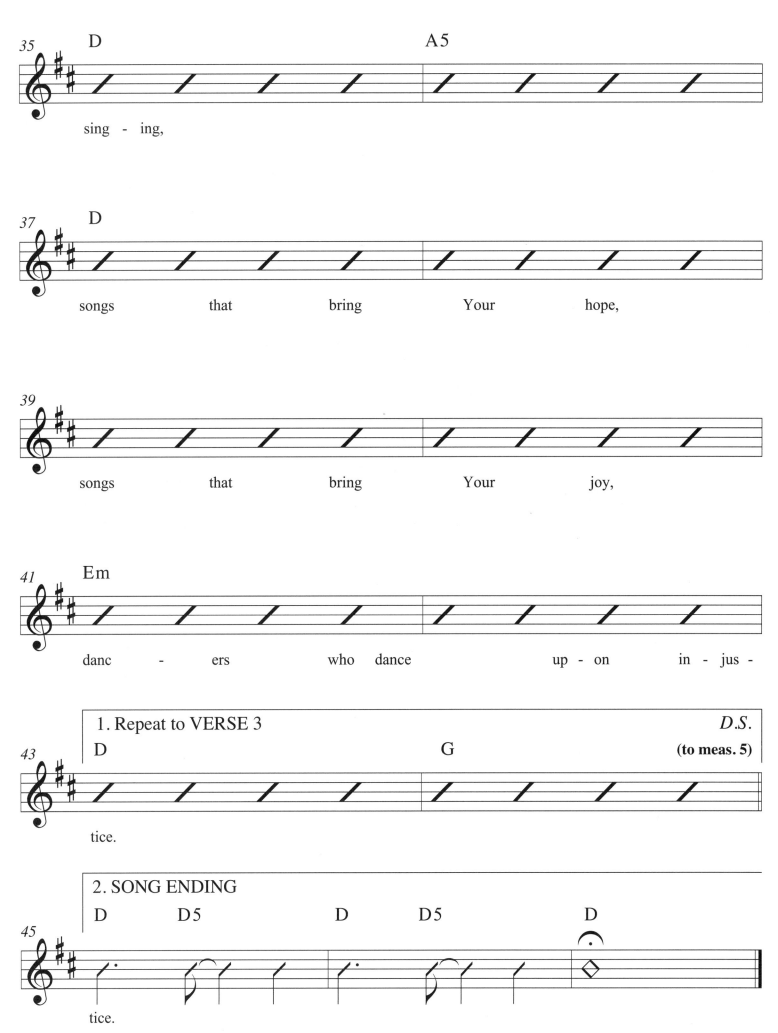

In Christ Alone

Words and Music by
STUART TOWNEND *and* **KEITH GETTY**

God of Wonders

Words and Music by
MARC BYRD *and* **STEVE HINDALONG**

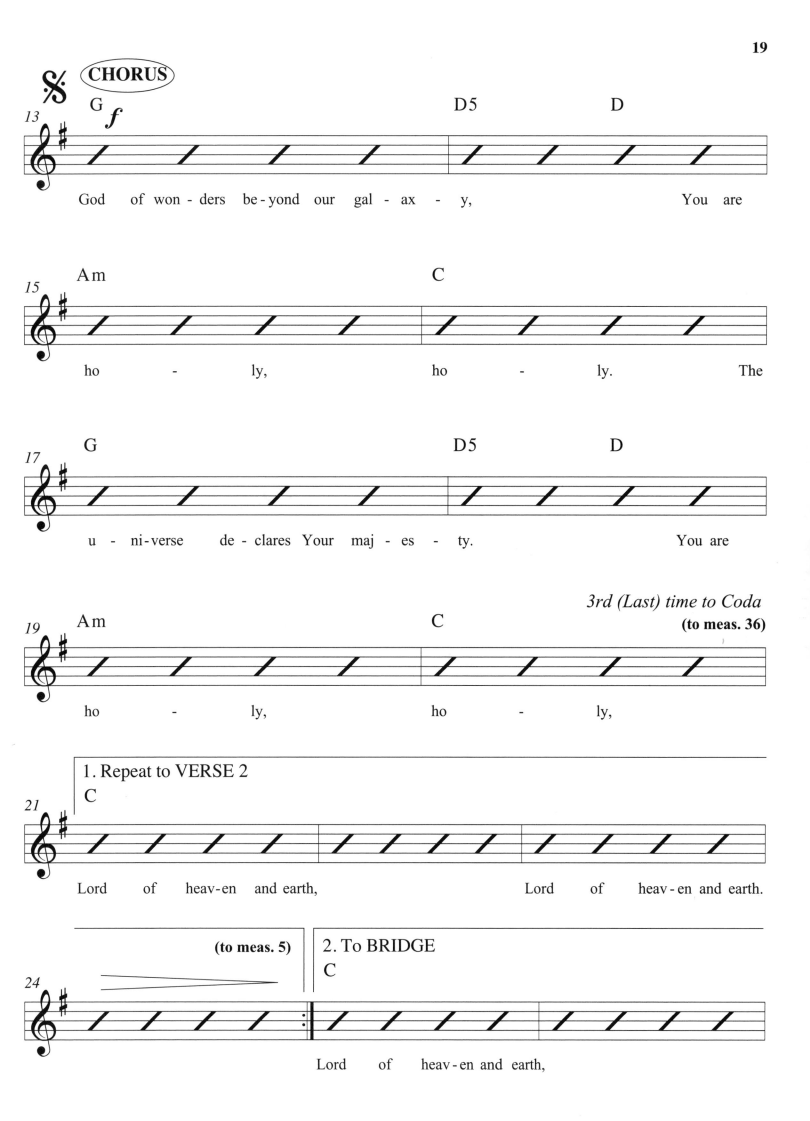

Here I Am to Worship

Words and Music by
TIM HUGHES

VERSES 1, 2

| G | D5 | Am | C |

1. Light of the World, You stepped down in - to dark - ness,
2. King of all days, oh, so high - ly ex - alt - ed,

| G | D5 | C |

o - pened my eyes, let me see
glo - rious in heav - en a - bove,

| G | D5 | Am | C |

beau - ty that made this heart a - dore You,
hum - bly You came to the earth You cre - at - ed,

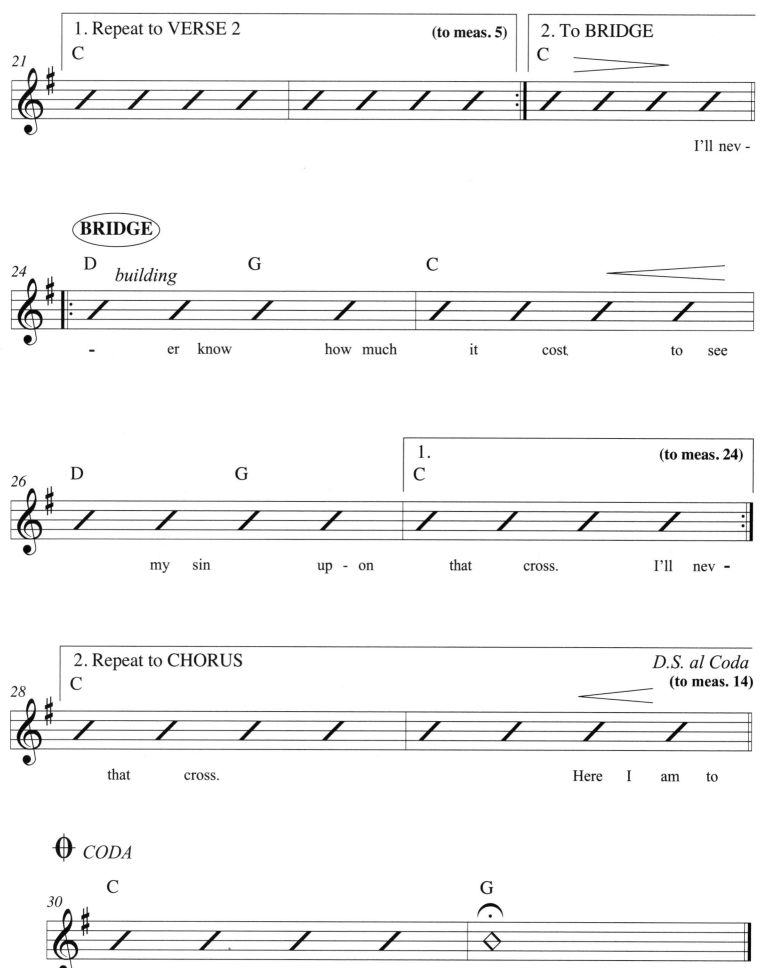

You Are My All in All

Words and Music by
DENNIS JERNIGAN

VERSES 1, 2

1. You are my strength when I am weak. You are the treas-ure that I
2. Tak-ing my sin, my cross, my shame, ris-ing a-gain, I bless Your

seek. You are my all in all.
name. You are my all in all.

Seek-ing You as a pre-cious jewel, Lord, to give up I'd be a
When I fall down, You pick me up; when I am dry, You fill my

fool. You are my all in all.
cup. You are my all in all.

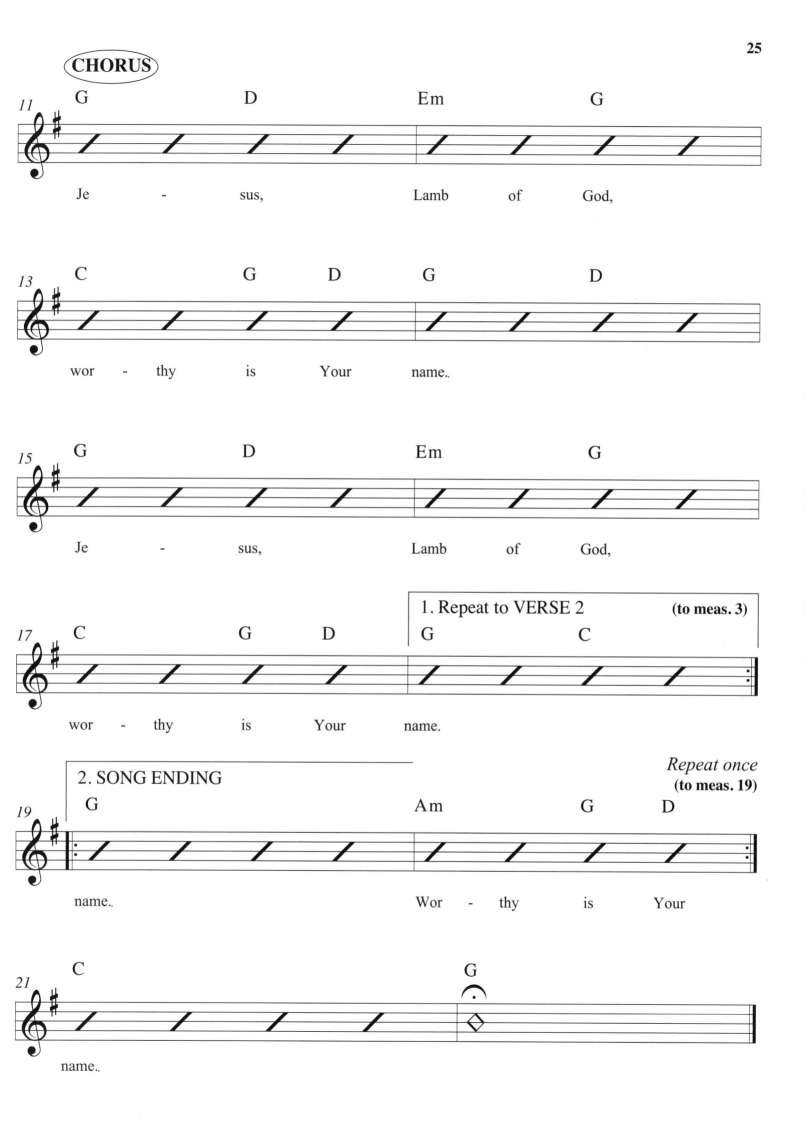

Let God Arise

Words and Music by
CHRIS TOMLIN,
ED CASH *and* **JESSE REEVES**

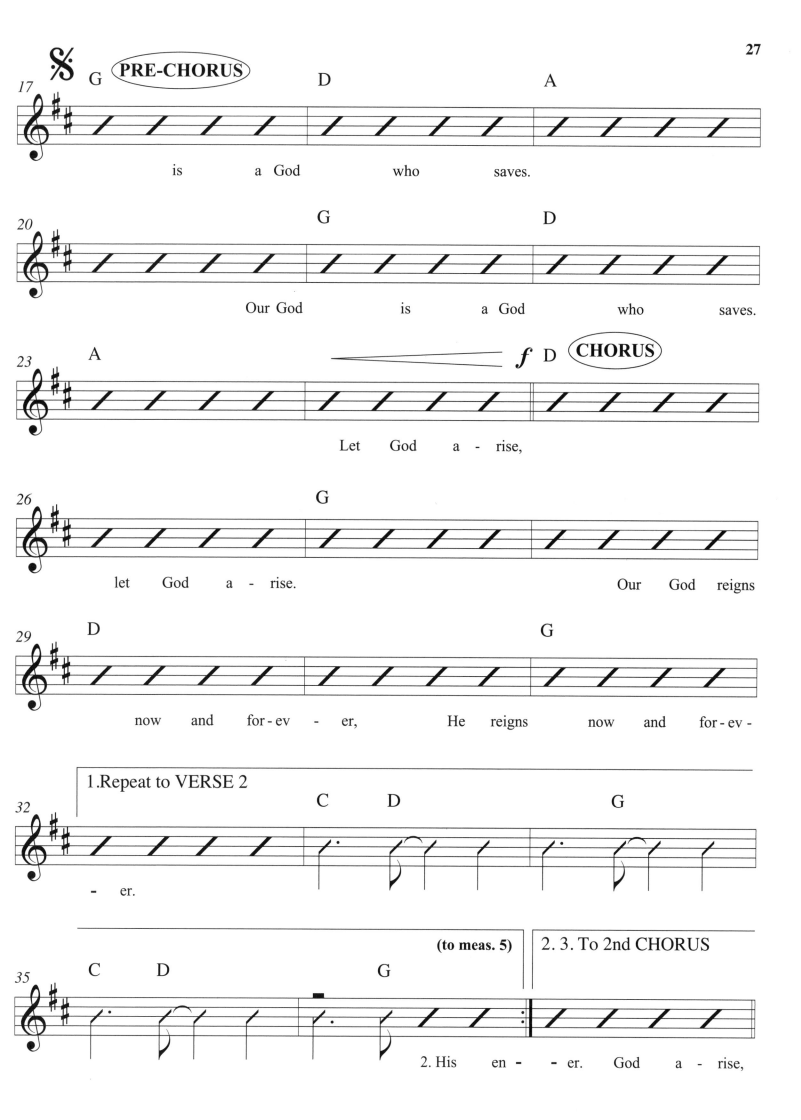

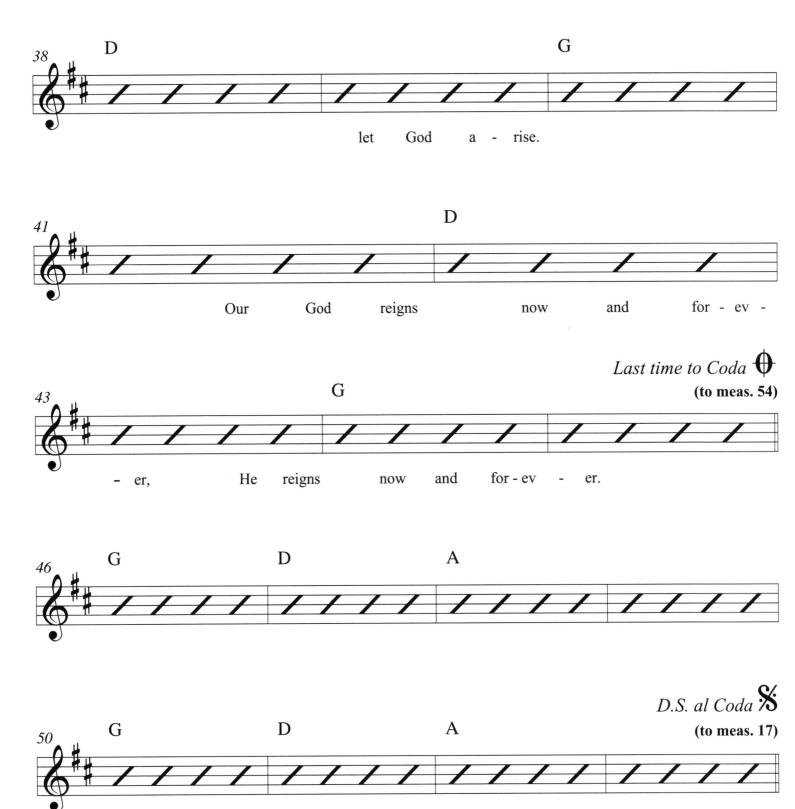

D   **G**

38

let   God   a - rise.

D

41

Our   God   reigns   now   and   for - ev -

Last time to Coda ⨁
(to meas. 54)

G

43

- er,   He   reigns   now   and   for - ev - er.

G   **D**   **A**

46

D.S. al Coda 𝄋
(to meas. 17)

G   **D**   **A**

50

Our God

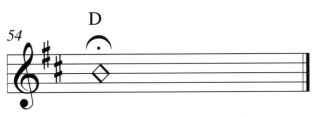

⨁ *CODA*

D

54

The Wonderful Cross

Words and Music by
JESSE REEVES,
CHRIS TOMLIN and **J. D. WALT**

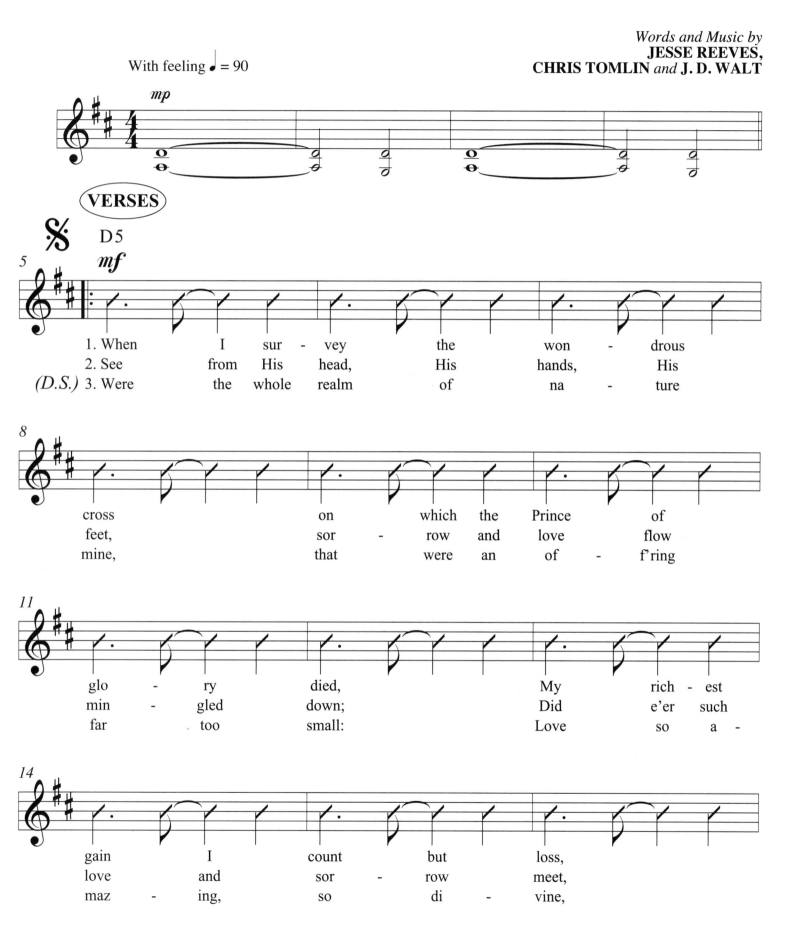

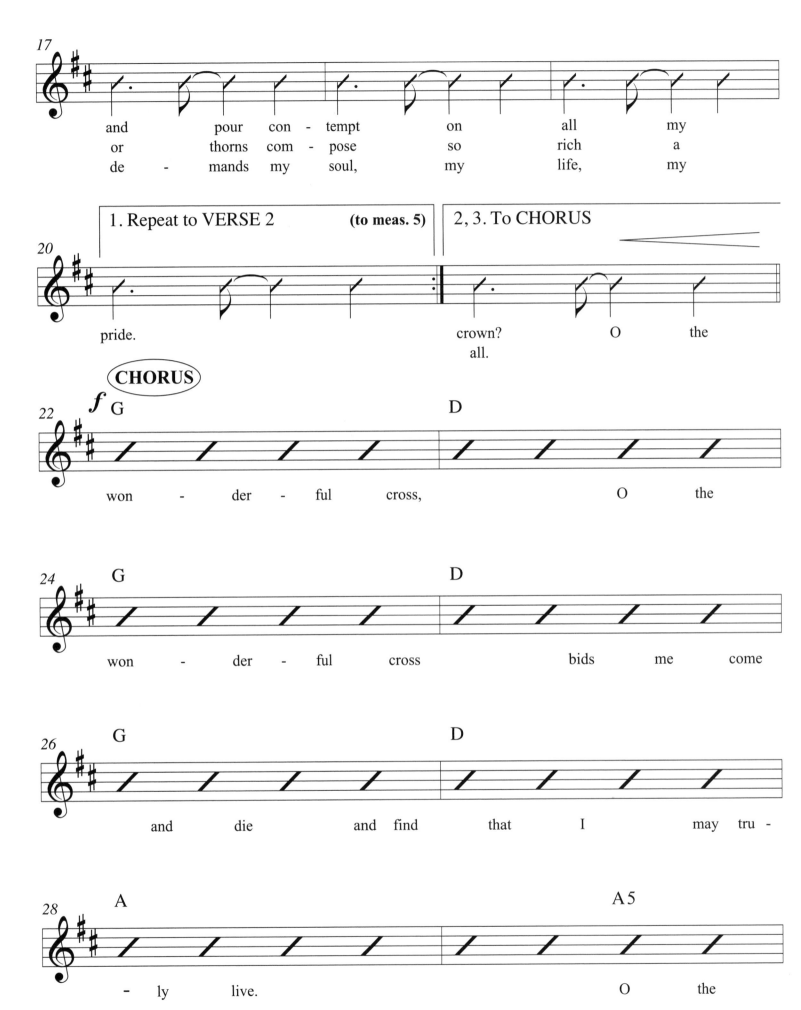

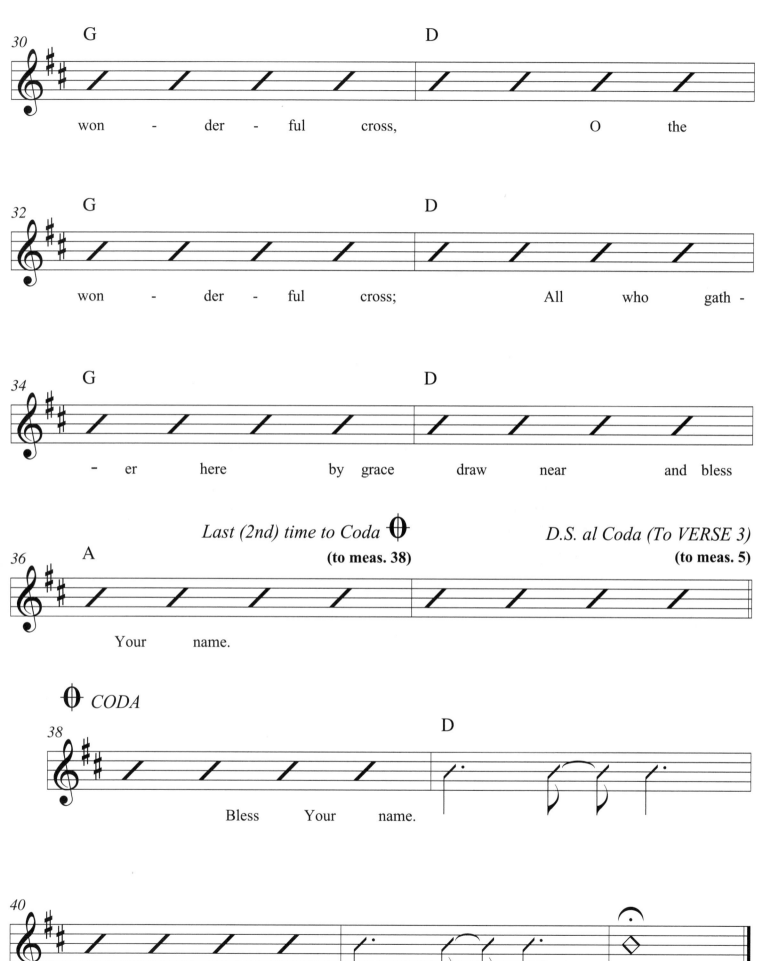

LEARN GUITAR WITH A PRO!

DVD INCLUDED!

GUITAR
PRAISE & WORSHIP
Level One

LEARN TO PLAY GUITAR WITH SONGS OF PRAISE

Shawnee Press, Inc.
Nashville, TN 37212

Learn to play guitar with songs of praise and worship!

Guitar Praise and Worship – Level One will have you playing guitar fast! This method is designed for the beginning guitarist who wants to join the praise band…or play at home…or for friends…or for just about any "gig" around. It's designed to get you on the fast track to strumming songs right away. Written by renowned Nashville studio session guitarist and teacher John Pell, *Guitar Praise and Worship – Level One* is a unique, fresh and *fun* approach to learning how to play guitar. The enclosed DVD features the author leading you through lessons and tips…as if you are sitting with him for a lesson in his private studio. The Bonus Chapters on the DVD contain special practice tracks to build your "chops" even more! There are also great tips included in the book on being in or starting a praise band. Get started playing and praising today…with *Guitar Praise and Worship*.

SB1045 • Book/DVD Combo • $29.95